OCTOBERS

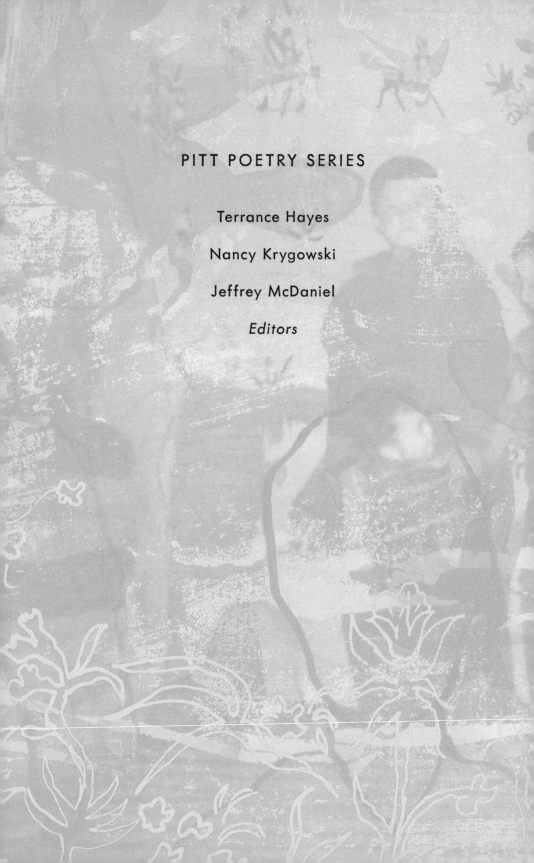

PITT POETRY SERIES

Terrance Hayes

Nancy Krygowski

Jeffrey McDaniel

Editors

OCTOBERS

SAHAR MURADI

UNIVERSITY OF PITTSBURGH PRESS

This book is the winner of the 2022 Donald Hall Prize for Poetry, awarded by the Association of Writers and Writing Programs (AWP). AWP, a national organization serving more than three hundred colleges and universities, has its headquarters at George Mason University, Mail Stop 1E3, Fairfax, VA 22030.

The Donald Hall Prize for Poetry is made possible by the generous support of Amazon.com.

Published by the University of Pittsburgh Press, Pittsburgh, Pa., 15260
Manufactured in the United States of America
Printed on acid-free paper
10 9 8 7 6 5 4 3 2 1

ISBN 13: 978-0-8229-6708-8
ISBN 10: 0-8229-6708-1

Cover art: Detail from Saadia Batool's *A Thread to Map a Route*, 2022. Mixed media on canvas, 11 × 16 in.

Cover design: Alex Wolfe

For Nico—in the depths, in the vastness, with utter delight

Here is the month of straw. Paper
the body who blew away. The one who
made the world over. The ones who splintered
it. Month of the harvest and growing ground-
less. The gut-comb. I was a one before
October and I became another
after.

CONTENTS

IV. THE BIRTH, 2018

V. AFTER OCTOBER

OCTOBERS

I. THE OCCUPATION, 2001

The Picture Tin

Father learned exile by television
And this was wartime.
Mother washed. I sat quietly with a tin
Full of pictures. Night drew.
My hands grew warm touching their faces
In youth.

There was a roll of bills
in a pocket in the closet
But why had she shown it to me?
Mother's hands made rough
sounds on her uniform.
It was green
Like the tips of my eyes, now bedtime.

The corners I touched felt like tusks.
"We say *elephant tears*," he once said.
In my picture tin
The war raged on: black and white
A fugitive zebra on the street
With my heart pulsing red in its mouth.

Salam Alaikum

Salam alaikum
Once, when I was a girl

I ni sógóma
I believed in morning,
like a hot, yellow apple

Manda nabaasheyn
We never tired. Father said,
God is good

Héré sira
We slept in twos and threes

Famil chatoor ast
It was a matter of everyone

Sómógó bédi
Someone had work, someone didn't
Someone always offered something

Owlada khoob astan
We were kids but we knew everything
We belonged to everyone

I sigi na
After prayer, there was tea
After tea, there was fruit

Befarmayen
Mother taught us to draw our feet
To let others go first

Aw ni tile
In time, day gave way to night

Jan-e tan jor ast
Someone would show up asking for my body
Then another

I dógó cé ka kéné
We would exchange brothers
who were not our brothers

Khudaya shukur
The earth met us in different ways
For some, it rained
For others, there wasn't water for the stones

A barika Allah ye
We thanked God for blessing us
and not our neighbors

Khuda hafiz
History was the first to leave
and without a trace

Aw ni wula
Father said the night has hands
Mother reminded me of the apple

Shab bakhair
In the dark
I held nothing

A Secret Life in Misspelled Cities

Kabul

There was once. I remember. I think it must have been there. Just imagine.

Bamiyan

I climbed your two vacuums and lost my breath. But I did not cry, seeing the women in the field balance pots on their wisdom bumps.

Wardak

Malalai was taking me home. "There will be apple orchards," she said. "And fighting," laughed the driver, who was armed. I told him I was not scared, as we hemmed the narrow mountainside to the sound of something I could not name.

Paghman

There is no explanation for it. No science or natural law. The story goes that if you take a single brick from this city, no scorpion will ever sting you. Father says, we kept ours with your mother's gold.

Mazar

1

Just stepping into the square, into the standing blue pool under the pulse of a thousand white wings, something happened. Something loosened, fell, or passed through me: a precision, a shudder, lightning, vivid as a heartbreak.

2

It's true, I had a crush on the malang at the shrine, who marched in rags and tassels with a tail of children, calling, "Allah hu, Allah hu, Allah hu." His hand never extended, but all of him untethered.

3

Better than a man: tarashak on a hot a day.

Qargha

1

We were three in the back in black scarves that were dusted white by the time we got there. And seeing the old hotel for the first time in twenty-five years, father, whose corners are always straight, confessed a drunken boyhood.

2

Please don't tell anyone that we left work early that day and drove to the lake and ate kabobs and sour cherries and I lowered my scarf, being one with two beards and families peppered about and joy still in bad taste that I tried to be small, but there was the water just like that, wide and rare and like Florida, a clear sheet of possibility, and the whisper started, the itch spread, and grew and ballooned, and before I knew it—I leapt in—with everything on and with all abandon.

Panjsher

1

The difference between a poem and a lion is an alphabet. The difference between five poems and five lions is slight.

2

We walk to the hilltop that watches over the valley. We remove our shoes and continue to water his hands, now that he is under a green hat.

3

We creep past the stones marked white for mines. We kneel and spread out our picnic. An ant, a shoe, a rocket—all of it suddenly level.

words by which to tell time

صلح

peace

a word that ends silently

a word whose feet never touch the ground

۳۸ سال

38 years

not unlike

۳۰ اشک سال

thirty tears old

بیوه

widow

could be

بی

without

و

and

without *and*

without her *and*

her conjunction

the coincidence of two heavenly bodies
at the same celestial longitude

بيوه

without her heavenly half

2 million

بيوه

2 million halves

in heaven

سلاح

weapon

so near

صلح

how one might

use one

for the other

as in *drone*

for *lull*

bomb

a word that ends silently

a word whose feet never touch the ground

here

بمب

a word with a tail

in another country

a tail that lands clearly, firmly

a sound that splits

their mouths

Mariposa

We flew out of San Jose and you told me
about the butterfly farm. You said they only
live between a few hours and a month. That
they weave cocoons of golden thread, which
look like a lady's earring. That when they drop
it, the first thing they do is defecate. That they
already know how to fly. That their bright
colors rub off on your hand like a lady's eye
shadow. That the monarch's orange color is
poison. You said, can you believe it, you see
them and you never think.

We flew over Cuba and I told you
about the butterfly farm. I said they
only live an hour. That they weave cocoons of
invisible thread, which look like nothing.
That when they drop it, the first thing
they do is submit. That they already know
how to survive. That their bright colors
rubbed off like a lady's lipstick. That
the subject's orange color is poison.
I said, can you believe it, you don't see them
so you never think about them.

A Recovery of the Disappeared

1
Start with the palms of your hands
Find the faintest branch

2
Take your fourth fingers
Touch them to your thumbs
Feel how unused they are

3
Remember the small of your lip
Where your breath gathers
It still gathers

4
Notice how your hand fits your neck
Your neck your hand
Think of your neck in boyhood
Its hairs rising with a kiss
Tender as a baby toe

5
Do not think of your baby

6
Study your nails
How they return consistently
How the body affirms itself
Consistently

7

Trace your navel
Your nipple
The net of your manhood
These are your beginnings

8

Reckon your blinking
How many per minute
How many per hour
Did you ever think how many times in your life
And empty of your will?
That is what your father meant by God

9

Do not think of your father

10

See the veins on the backs of your hands
In the alleys of your arms
No city moves as fast

11

Remember your body in the ocean
Rising and falling
Rising and falling
Being taken against yourself
Being submerged
Removed from the sun
Far from sound
Remember the panic
Remember how the ocean did not panic

12

Feel the hollow of your foot
The small roof it makes
A tunnel for the ants
Those beads of dedication
They know nothing of leaving
Of closing the sail
Lower your gaze

washee / was she

she was *washee* i told her you are
like your motherland a wilderness
needs a belt laid down two white
hotel towels took her into the tub to
wudu the boys out of her mouth pointed
her nipples toward *qibla* wiped clean
her intention to perform *ruk'u* as if
carrying a glass of *chai* on her back
fold at the knees palms to the ground
tucked her soles under her *astaghfirullah*
used country

in my used country i felt his teeth
circle as a mosquito the black mystery
he placed my *right* hand over my wrong
stain said he was bringing me *home*
offered me a suite with a lock a key in
the shape of a *brother* perhaps twenty-
two years old my body *pure* as a glass
table he spilled *was she* my boss on my
back at night came easy as a fly
to post-conflict *faithfully*
used my country

come baby

we come carrying crying
the train of colors from the sky
come breathing clutching
what few what fierce
come climbing in plastic
shoes a desert a white flag
come baby a bag of fluid
come baby come baby come
brother even the dog
wants a cigarette even
the smoke wants to be free

Retreat

a word is legged,
      armed

to *retreat*, move back
from a forward or threatened position
      as in chess, a piece

to *withdraw*, leave
to remove or take away
      as in love

"the whole country being a swamp
      a labor of time and utility"
      (Lady Sale, Caboul, 1842)

the longest war
      the definition
of a quagmire
      (Washington, 170 years later)

the going into
and coming out of
      a home
      a body

as in a bog

she noted, "remarkable
from having a few trees
      and a grave or two under them"

citing Alexander
          & co.
late books, headlines
          "The Graveyard of Empires"

as in literature
a pretty banner

          in a village called
The Husbandless
          "we were heavily fired upon"

which is "a curious complex"

          said Brzezinski
"they don't like foreigners with guns
 in their country"

as in
          someone must

Zuihitsu for the New Diaspora

In Cornwallville, thinking of Kabul. The hush of new snow—and leafless. Balkh, Bamiyan, Herat. Jalalabad with its orange blossoms necklaced on a thread. The girls had given it to me that spring. Now a bookmark. The blue light of winter morning. Icicles on red berries. I watched them fall.

We drive to keep the baby asleep. Wet firewood, wild turkeys, a ring-necked pheasant. Mistaking hunting posts for tree houses, a wooden stag for new life.

G. wrote, *your language is home.* Each morning I trace my evictions.

N. finally crosses the border. Eighty-five hours by bus. A wife and four children. His press pass buried in his father's yard. Nangarhar—Kandahar—Quetta— Karachi—Peshawar. Goes to Saturn to get to Venus. Dirt roads and forged papers. Two five-minute piss stops. Bribes the size of windows. A car accident. Pneumonia in his newborn. He is thirty-one. Hair frosted.

My memories begin at age nine. Before that, a long, white expanse, mute as a rope.

Nothing is quiet about small towns with their hateful lawn signs.

New York to Florida and back. I come of age along a corridor. Gregory. Linton. Hawthorne. Vanderbilt. Each move cleans the tongue. Circle becomes *sare-kal.* Bald head.

All my life trying to name the thing without naming it.

Father's laugh rises from a wound. Every year, on the day, the tease: "Your birth was a curse." The year of my arrival twinned with the Soviets'. It's August. I stroke the taut lampshade of my belly. A black band bisecting it. A flag. Soon, my son, his own twinning: the end of an occupation and its harsh exit.

Who will I be once the gates open? To have to learn anew: the latch, the loop, and how lonesome. I want to be multiple, a hologram, slippery as a foal.

In a snow globe shaken violently. A thousand points of undoing. To be unmoored repeatedly. Torn from a soft, knit blanket. From this distance, most color is out of reach. Just the wide blue gape of disbelief.

The "witching hour" is apparently the baby's effort to process the day's information. A system overloaded. The roar of life through a thimble.

Welcome. Language laughs back. *Opportunity.* Who wants to leave? asks Z. *Allies.* Who wants to be a spore?

Sitting by the East River, in the sun. Trying to recover a new leaf, a stem, some anchoring green in this skeletal season. On the bridge, pigeons. Tercets of bubblegum feet mapping an arc.

At last, someone comes to salt the path. To scatter and seed, to lengthen the radius from home.

II. THE PASSING, 2016

Just Before 88-30 51ˢᵗ Avenue

—when he squeezed into the trunk of an orange
Flickswagoon on an otherwise ordinary night

—when she began her goodbyes, threading them
astah astah across the year, knowing, not-knowing

—when he arrived in northern Virjinyaw and hurried out,
the failure of his mouth against the street signs

—when she made her way alone from Kabul
to Peshawar with three kids in rags, passing

—when he followed his qaum to a speared skyline
and the equalizing grace of a subway, color-coded

—when she was stuck in Colombo, daily checking
the consulate, bargaining to eat, to not look back

—when the Amrikai said it's been *issued*, but she didn't
know and cried against the alien prick of the word

—when they finally finally finally ۴۰۰ days
later at JFK wept and the youngest said, who are you

—when they arrived at the brick face of REGORY HALL,
the G ghosted long ago, at last at home amongst the lost names

Typical Fish

father is on the tongue
of the sewing machine
above him a plastic placemat
of fish a pink one
a pinker
a black and white

just gonna lift you a little
Tom says
like we do everyday

typical fish

his hands on his
hips and heaves
father's naked accent

Tom used to live in New York City

used to work in the market
used to stuff them with rocks
so they'd weigh more
so the women would pay more

in the Village to be exact

father's two stickers
two black glyphs
x's or t's or what's that
number just right and left
of your bone hive
two eyes on the plastic waterfall

the Israelis are dropping
leaflets
let's leave
Tom says before

father's a channel
of peppercorns
bisected by a green line
on a skewer of time

is Veselka still there

in a screen the size of a village
someone is lying still

know what the safest street is 3rd Street know why

we couldn't get the picture
so we took NPR down Haverhill
right into the parking lot of St. Mary's
FOX at the waiting room

I heard weighting room
he heard fish scales
but we couldn't get the picture

father asked me if I knew what it meant
Peshmerga

Tom lined him up exactly
x's and o's and oh we had better go
for peace was dropping

your father's a good man they don't make anymore

fish eyes
for when you cry

no I didn't know

in the waiting room
father dubbed the glyphs
peh yaw sheen meem ray gawf hay
pesh for early
merga for death

Hell's Angels that's why

Rattling

1

Who is this boy in the bone sac asking what to do? See his thin kite whipping.
Trembling skin over his eyes. What is he asking that we should know. Young grass at his
feet.

Suppose the king is a failing leaf. His wife a blade of glass.

What should I do, she asks, rattling.

2

Once, on the tarmac, among the cadavers of green tanks, military planes, the
mountains encircling them, he kissed the black earth. It had been twenty-five years.
Time hurried down his face. Clear, not clear, clear. Men elbowing over the bags. Here,
brother, let me. One came smoothly, is that you, my brother, do you remember me, I
am in a bad way. Again he became a boy caught by the weather, gave his arms, handed
out his eyes, and kissed the stranger with a golden bill.

3

Let her be a boat. And the sea dark, rummaging.

4

Bending to tie her lace, she is halved by the dialogue between pearls. Let her be a boat within a boat: two boats spilling water.

5

Peonies trapped in their pink fists, each of the three daughters had different faces. Their eyes sounded.

One sent invitations the color of fatigue, one prodded the door with science, one stayed on the shore,

singing *I have a mother better than a blade of grass / friends better than flowing water*

6

He placed his faith neatly in a handshake that belonged to a body outside of him. What can you do for me. Please, she asked, what can you do for him. And swallowed her pearls. Two sacs rattling.

The handshake had done something before for him. Had built a cathedral made of calendars. Three hundred thousand pages held his body up. The way the sun glinted, you could not see the words.

Take away the enormous seeing. Please.

7

They go to the shrine, tie the cloth, distribute the flour, stand alongside a mother beating her chest, a child with two unused snakes, eyes rolling inside, a black box, seven circles, the desert, water to the elbows, barefoot, head to the stone.

The screen, a window, half legible, enter the girls.

8

Who is this soft peach in a Hurricanes cap, glasses begging for an arrow? Doesn't he know? When he shares his skeleton, a blackbird with red wings becomes a red-winged blackbird.

9

Neither had learned to swim, all those years on the peninsula. When the storms came rattling, they would shutter the windows and squeeze into the closet.

They would fasten to the radio.

On the two-legged thread of Florida's 717

She tells us about the 3-day donkey ride from Peshawar to Jalalabad
to bury her mother.

Father tells me to slow down,
to let the truck pass.

She says she had white Nikes
that poked out from under her chadri.

"I was a sight."
"There are lots of cops," he warns.

"You can't see them."
It's a warm black all around us.

Kaka Najib quiet in the back,
watching the years.

"Money was different then," she says.
"Ten dollars became a fistful. It was a hard year."

Twenty-two days between her brother and her mother.
It was heartbreak.

Just let them pass, he says.
In the mirror   everything doubles.

Jan / Jahan

he is not here
was here

was just
Here

was just

a bloom
of eyes dark

ening

I held some
once

once

a Padar
jan

I had a one
say,
jan-e-Padar

Once

some one
to sum

All

jahan-e-Padar

Padar:
jahan

Facsimile

My father was an idea from Afghanistan. From Kabul. From Chindawol. Home of the Qizilbash. The red-hatted. The crimson-crowned. A balloon in twelve parts. One for each imam.

In my mind,

I trace your bony cheek.

Two bumps of earlobe.

God is as close

as the soft of the ear.

Photographs erupt:

The long space

in my eyes.

Had I known them. Or how to lay my head on the stone. To drop my arms at my side in prayer. Had I known how they'd wash his body. Or that only the men could carry him. Or how to wail like a good woman. How to answer when they said "zindagi saret bashad." May life keep over you.

I rubbed your feet

under the sky blue blanket.

Six blankets.

The oval of your mouth,

drying.

We took turns.

The yellow sponge.

Your teeth

in the styrofoam

cup.

Wouldn't it have been different if I were not in these un-United States? If family were not marbles scattered. If I hadn't grown up so far from the community. A community. So lacking of a net, that I mirrored my father in his interiority, in his unsettledness in his own being. Wouldn't it have been entirely different had we remained in Afghanistan? In so many ways, of course. And yet, somehow, wouldn't we have lost so much less? Wasn't that what he was always saying, circling the wormhole of his regrets?

His regrets coupled with romance the way exile courts imagination. What could have been. What should have. And shadows the present. On *if only's* he raised a family.

You that what?

That once?

That long?

That should forever?

You what?

You—my.

Irrelevant—all.

I keep coming back.

Faithfully.

To empty.

Had he not left Kabul. Had he not left New York. Had he not worked like a dog. Had they not left us long hours to work like dogs. Had we spoken right, dressed right. Had we not left for school. Had we returned home. Had we married right. Had he not smoked, drank, gambled, faced Qibla so late in life. Had we ever faced Qibla.

Had he not wished into the vacuum of his own father. Had his father touched him except with the back of his hand. Had he not worked for his father. Had he not worked for him for free. Had he not watched his father bring women to the house. Had he not watched his mother draw them baths and serve them tea. Had he himself, with his beautiful bride, not frantically checked behind the doors of their new home. Had he not left his home to squeeze into the trunk of a Volkswagen in the dead of night. Had he not crossed so many borders to freedom. Had freedom not meant becoming a dog to new masters.

"Why do we blush before death?"

Trauma is a door simultaneously open and shut.

It's true—I saw you shy.

Father had few words. But for history. Ours, that towered, that he declaimed, and in doing, had me at his feet, awing. Bactria. Khorasan. Timurlang. Taking notes, recording his voice. At his feet, making kites. Bowing the bamboo as he glued the tissue paper. Marveling at how he folded the sheet upon itself, cut an almond eye, and revealed a daisy. How he chose his colors: red, black, and green.

He could not name a color I liked.

Today, I am wearing you.

Your peyran, waaskat.

Your traditional

shirt and vest.

The color of khaak.

It is a cold wind at my back.

Constant. A kind of

draft. Severed

again.

As if Afghanistan.

Dari.

The stories.

Poetry. As if

every stream of news.

Every mud brick.

Of history (ours).

Is no longer (mine).

Love and fear, our twin occupants. His tender voice, its glassy edges. Persian poetry and Qur'anic verse that fountained out of him. Histories and myths that bloomed on his tongue. The hours he disappeared before the television with bottle. His voice pelting at my mother, my brother. The alien parts that commanded all reverence: the pair of knobs at the door of his left ear; his low, cascading eyebrows we'd cut monthly; the ghosted nails of his fifth toes. His growing and rightful tirades against this country that degraded him, that spit on his crooked mouth, his wrong skin and faith. Work that stole his body and steeled his rage.

Today is your birthday.

Your legal birthday.

Not your true calendar.

According to the law.

Which did not accord you

much.

I was seized when he punched our angry neighbor, the cop, noting that the Soviet army had never conquered him, why should he fear a mere badge.

My wide eyes widened.

And why can't the image

not be the hospital?

And why couldn't your mouth close?

That she wrapped you with gauze

—so much white gauze—

and so tightly,

forcefully,

around your chin.

A child

again.

She said custom.

The indignity.

Forcing your body

for the living.

But was it,

just like that?

Had you been

and then suddenly not?

Was that your boat untethered?

Was it you?

Or wasn't it?

The jaw locking.

Who was it

who wasn't?

Justice eludes. My father had had only one example from history: Dr. William Brydon, the alleged sole survivor of the Afghan massacre of 16,000 British troops and civilians during the First Anglo-Afghan War in 1842. Brydon was let go to tell the tale of the British defeat. When I was in college, my father had me track down Lady Butler's "Remnants of an Army," the 1879 painting of this broken, beaten man on a limping horse. He asked for a large, color photocopy to frame.

He was, again, enigmatic. And my hunger fattened.

I wore you.

To near you.

To approximate the shade of your ear.

I was almost there. Yes,

I was there

in the hollow.

He—his universe—became the nucleus of my writing. The writing itself a test: how many courses in his alphabet, however haltingly. That he should respond with looseleaf letters and birthday cards inscribed with his free, raw script. Beautiful and illegible. I labored to discern and be revealed to. To near him. In Afghanistan the alphabet-illiterate pay someone to read their letters and documents. In New York, I would do the same.

The family tree.

The table now.

With its missing legs.

The papers.

Your letters I could not—.

Years deciphering.

Our numbers

beginning with cipher.

The oval

of your mouth,

drying.

So many years I waited for those jeweled papers to reveal a question, to ask me
something, specifically about me, my life. About my childhood wall of male artists, my
adolescent despair with knife in hand, my short-lived jobs and quick moves. My poetry.

Or had he known I was just a reflecting pool?

The stacks

and stacks

and unfinished

and

your voice

like a harbor.

I leaned to impress. Read the news to recite. Studied our history to repeat. Storied our
roots there, our routes here. Collected photographs, conducted interviews, piled out-
of-print books. After college, I moved to Afghanistan. Begged that he return with me.
Beheld him weep on the plane passing into the airspace, touching the ground. The
entire airplane of exiles erupting into tears.

Days with Madar.

Occupying this space together.

And differently.

As if

it's a single space.

As if

we are singular people.

Decades his eyes darting backwards. When he finally returned to Kabul, the garden was gone. What once was. What might have been. If only. His fingers hung in the air, mid-sentence. Nothing—no one—was recognizable or left or not hungry. His childhood home flattened and squatted by a poor family. Strangers looped his arms and feigned knowing him, for a dollar. The air enflamed his asthma. And he hurried back to Florida. All those years, looking back. Suddenly, at last, he straightened his neck.

He planted flowers, bougainvillea, bright and wild, in the yard.

Tried praying again.

Something of consistency.

Of beyond-human.

Of surrender.

Guidance.

Of nearing you.

Your face is receding behind the ordinary day.

His knuckles softened. And soon flowers rioted. Across his body. In his esophagus. War, exile, trauma anglicized as cancer. I hurried home from Kabul and saw my myth tangled in tubes. Was it true—could my father be mortal?

And where are you?

Over me?

Beside me?

In a pattern of light

on the white wall?

Where do you reside?

Exactly?

For two years I worked at the Foreign Ministry that he should thrill a Qizilbash enter with her head high. I had gone for his approval, his kiss on my forehead. Or maybe I stayed out of surrogacy. To do what he was doing: to repent with my body. Two years into the American occupation, a wash of artillery and aid, excess and poverty, hard and soft violences. The borders blurred: I was the country men—native and foreign—kept trying to rescue, tame, conquer. Like a good mujahid, I played every role. And like a good shahid, I renounced myself.

Any moment.

Rises up.

A well.

A wave.

An unfathomable plunge.

Every chance I had, I ran home. And at his feet again, with my cup outstretched. Maybe a line from Hafiz, an aya on the glory of God, his story about the haunted hotel in Mazar-e-Sharif. An afternoon or two bandaging kites. Most days watching his eyes close early on the couch, his gaze suspend in the sliding glass. The privilege of massaging his bones.

Yesterday marching.

I would have run to you after.

All these days.

We would have been clicking our tongues,

shaking our heads at this fool.

You would have compared him to ones there.

Dostum?

Hekmatyar?

One of old?

Timurlang's son

who blinded his brother?

We would have reviewed your pains.

One after the other.

You would have said:

jan-e Padar.

In the reckoning, he found his maker. And submitted daily. He sobered, kneeled, made Umrah—twice. In the rolling ellipse of white cloth, he was one. Among ones. His voice softened. He returned with a new face, eyes lifted of their shade.

Pride bored him, was of no use. Pride in country, ethnicity, history. His declamations thinned to a dialogue, intimate and holy.

The hollow of your cheeks,

for instance.

The further he went, the higher my mantle.

Hail at the window.

Glass chattering.

I take my face into the crowd.

Down Avenue A,

1ˢᵗ,

Houston.

The thing

widening.

So much writing is born of longing. So much living. All attachment thins to that lone jewel: to near and be neared. As a child, one's survival, like a plant's, depends on looking up, on a greater radiance and warmth, on a deep fastening.

No one knows.

No one knows exactly.

You.

Cut out of.

When are you going to stop writing about your father, another writer asks.

Your face appears.

The faintness of your voice.

You are building a kite.

How to repair the hole

in the tissue paper.

You paste a piece

over a piece.

And let go.

My father had only ever been an idea.

III. THE SEPARATION, 2009

Begin

Start with your hand behind my ear
The cradle of your question
Quiet as a hairline crack

Start with the moment before the fall
A pant the size of the first story
And eyes of the oldest appetite

What is wider than that leaning?
Vaster than that request?

Start with our two sets of hands and legs and lips
Searching for the source
Like Rimbaud pursuing spiders in her neck

How deeply will we look?
How generously will we reveal?

Start with the low hum across the body
The faintest sound on the longest journey
Not the word, but the blood of the word

Start from here
Begin with this

Two Mountains

The silver warrant of your eyes
Two mountains breaking words
I would meet you in a fold of desire the sound of a skyline
reddening

So when did our house begin to lose its humor?
How did we end up in the attic?
Your face repeating in a collection of jars on the sill
Or is it mine?

Once, I knew so much less
of us
Half-moons on a nail would surprise
There were still faint stars to discover
in the minarets of my legs
the domes of your shoulders

There were no clocks
No night or day

Weren't we once infinite?
Flowers tiled endlessly

Didn't we bend our bodies
in the direction of something unfathomable
unfettered
Something as foolish as seeking?

Brink

A: Where would you like to start?
B: The telephone.

A: Where would you like to start?
B: In my Halloween costume: a cowgirl.

A: Where were you?
B: Hester Street.

A: Where were you?
B: My lunch break.

A: Where was he?
B: Madrid, with his father.

A: Where was he?
B: The telephone.

A: What did he say?
B: I cannot.

A: What did he say?
B: The pinhead root of a tornado.

A: What did you say?
B: Glass.

A: What did you say?
B: (my body)

A: What did you do?
B: My bandana was red.

A: What did you do?
B: I returned to the party.

A: What did you see?
B: The white blinding.

A: What did you see?
B: Pac-man and his ghosts.

"Discoveries have much more to do with dying continuously."

"Meet an open-ended question that has no conceptual answer."

"So the next time you encounter [ ], consider yourself lucky."

A: Where would you like to start?
B: I called Customer Service. I could do $29.99 a month for 500 minutes, free nights and weekends, or $39.99 a month for 500 minutes plus text, first he must call and release my number, keep two separate accounts under separate names, billing addresses, he remains the primary account holder, I will need a credit check.

A: Where would you like to start?
B: I called Customer Service. I should go online when I have a new address, update my individual billing for my student loans, credit card, bank accounts, work, retirement, insurance, doctor, dentist, gynecologist, life insurance, airline miles, magazine subscriptions, donations, tell all my friends and family, a mass email is a good option.

A: What did you do?
B: I bought binoculars.

A: What did you do?
B: The furniture.

A: What happened?
B: I couldn't stop.

A: What happened?
B: Seizures on the subway.

A: What did you do?
B: I bought four plants and named them.

A: What did you do?
B: I found a bookstore.

A: What did you get?
B: Fern, Totem, Jade, Banana.

A: What did you get?
B: "The trick is to not bail out."

A: What happened next?
B: I couldn't see my feet.

A: What happened next?
B: A flute in the refrigerator the size of Manhattan.

A: What was the weather like?
B: Glassy.

A: What was the weather like?
B: Everywhere.

A: What time was it?
B: Maybe it was time to eat.

A: What time was it?
B: There was no passage.

A: Where did you go?
B: My bed was tired.

A: Where did you go?
B: I needed arms.

A: Whom did you ask?
B: A room with twelve chairs.

A: Whom did you ask?
B: T. in Massachusetts.

A: What did they do?
B: They gave me a mirror and arms. They pointed to my feet.

A: What did they do?
B: They threw the light.

A: What did she do?
B: She was a nest of kind hair.

A: What did she do?
B: She stayed.

Staying

Leaning in

Going to the brink

Thanksgiving nobody
knew how to
it's not like somebody died
your reputation
how they hold their faces
first there was
and then
and now *you don't*
seem to get your culture
there was no word
for asking
for arms
We just want you
not to make another mistake

A: Where would you like to start?
B: I lost my hat.

A: Where would you like to start?
B: I found a bench and used the telephone.

A: What did you say?
B: He he he.

A: What did you say?
B: So much glass.

A: What did they say?
B: They said take the day off.

A: What did they say?
B: They would come; I needed them.

A: What did you say?
B: Yes, the students are fine.

A: What did you say?
B: I have a net among friends.

A: What happened?
B: The students were fine.

A: What happened?
B: I was being selfish. Who was I?

A: What happened next?
B: His body approached mine.

A: What happened next?
B: We went to see her one more time.

A: What did he say?
B: He said brother and sister.

A: What did he say?
B: Just brother and sister.

A: What did you say?
B: (my body) (my body!)

A: What did you say?
B: Glass.

A: What did he say?
B: Were you in a different room?

A: What did he say?
B: My amends.

A: What did you say?
B: I need a historical timeline.

A: What did you say?
B: Is it men?

December 7 home
to his boxes stacked
in the middle of the
room. His empty book-
shelf the middle book-
shelf. The note about
the computer. The li-
cense out in the open.
Our two countries start-
ing with the same letter.
The box marked "these
I don't want." His trash
in the bin. He had coffee
and chocolate. His hands
and his body, and he was
listening to *Rain Dogs*.

He is in the future.

Important to ask yourself

Choice of persons
Locations
Positions

And answer other than

Patience

Investigate your

Language of thanking
Ideas of causality
Ideals of spontaneity
The role of a long embrace

A: What happened?
B: His eyes were a tired army.

A: What happened?
B: He didn't say.

A: What did you say?
B: Who are you?

A: What did you say?
B: Just brother and sister?

A: What did he say?
B: A little sad.

A: What did he say?
B: I am sorry.

A: What did you say?
B: How do you hold your face?

A: What did you say?
B: Could he provide an ideogram of never with proper annotations?

A: What did she say?
B: When an animal surprises.

A: What did she say?
B: When an animal is taken by surprise.

"Self-deception becomes so skillfully and compassionately"

"We are not trying to solve a problem. We are not trying to make pain go
away or to become a better person. In fact, we are giving"

"Discursive thoughts are rather like wild dogs that need"

Into the lion's mouth . . .
may there be no flowers

A: Where would you like to start?
B: Echoes.

A: Where would you like to start?
B: I was a bird with tiny feet and small eyes, surviving from point to point.

A: Where were you?
B: I made notes.

A: Where were you?
B: I became bilingual.

A: What did you do?
B: I repeated things to myself.

A: What did you do?
B: I said yes to some and no to others, and sometimes I did not answer.

A: What did they say?
B: The door, it opened slowly.

A: What did they say?
B: Here is a rock to put in your pocket.

A: What did you do?
B: I asked to meet.

A: What did you do?
B: I asked never to meet.

A: What did he say?
B: "Hey" and other forms of mapping.

A: What did he say?
B: Sister.

A: What did you say?
B: The last time we kissed was October 16th.

A: What did you say?
B: (and shyly)

A: What did he say?
B: Powerless.

A: What did he say?
B: Thank you.

A: What did you say?
B: More than a window.

A: What did you say?
B: I was not there.

A: What did you do?
B: I went looking for my body.

A: What did you do?
B: Yes, my body!

Grasping

1

Time, I am leaning into you
pushing all my chips to your corners.
Here in the grief of my hands,
in the elegies of grasping,
remind me how useful it was,
the arrow.

2

Lessons of infancy:
When he leaves the room,
he does not exist.
If I am hungry,
I am permitted to wail.
And above my head, the mobile.
What finer constellations outside myself.

3

Echoes are inevitable.
The long space behind my body,
the tall stem of day hissing through the clock,
avoiding the gaps.
What does it mean to live in the gaps,
in the places where it is groundless,
to be so open
to this one morning with its distinct wink?

4

Something about surrender.
At dawn, a pledge of white flags.
Turning over what I cannot hold:
a library of nouns.
What courage it takes to admit one's size,
to polish the day over and over
grasping nothing.

A Separation

Every shattering narrow
A matter of kerning
i and *u*
Tracking changes in red alarm

Nothing is foul
when the cursor goes astray
We tried
and tired

IV. THE BIRTH, 2018

Reckoning

In the gray milk gaze of your beginning
I see the branches gather
Your first reckoning with light
its brimless hat, its unmitigated news
and an origin to wish back to

Now the branches are gathering
the shadows are passing
drumming mountains fitted with stars
made stars by the blush
of your soft balloon

Father is holding you
beholding your accordion
in fits of certain being
that shame the rest of us
in our having been
and outgrown the wonder

And all that is crooked
bone, sight, and sound
meets your pounding instrument
arching toward planted stars

Until everything shatters
with the squawk of a small pink urgent
and mother wolves you out
with white patience we remember

How your thousand faces
the far cells of your body flicker
like an athlete finding new meaning
you beg us back

night nursing

new hair in the round
to cup a brain quickening
seashell the still soft and unmade

*

asleep at the wheel
how to usher home
tiger on a tightrope

*

sometimes eyes open
sometimes excavation
her hands canvas

*

who saves whom
I crave her hunger
soften me please

*

rubber band arms
and other pithy epithets
I eat them all

*

she pushes and pulls at once
learns her lesson early
the heartbreak of desire

*

her arrows rise and fall
with the beat of pleasure
my appetite thickens

*

nothing stops our trysts
my body at war still waits for her knock
my General

*

I go to her fire in my throat
but my virus does not go
halo upon her mouth

*

the whiplash of her wheeze
cracks my midnight face
wakes open my every wrong

*

the steady pulling, pounding, squeezing
her urgency one day will disappear
she will forget how badly she wanted to live

*

she is clocking in again
almost on the hour
each time my white flag

*

we have to break it off
habit has corrupted need
rescue devoured response

*

my air has gone out of me
muscles dragging to her cage
my hair fanning limp at sea

*

are we complicit in the quiet outside this prayer
we are not each other's alone
we are alone

*

marvel at her starfish growing
the pinch, the press
and blue the sea of my doubts

*

I leave the room to lengthen her appetite
quick the cutlery of her cries
I gnaw the hand of my hesitation

*

my wrists weep
grey gloves to lift her
no one to lift me

*

she wants to meet earlier
more often, stay longer, harder
I hurry eyeless

*

the night before the office, before two
I am thinned beyond one
I want to lead for a change

*

my wants multiply
months fattening quietly
a new diamond in the room

*

this is getting rude
the hourly doorbell
my love can't buy time

*

when will I resume myself
when will she assume herself
I forget the night holds the day

*

Ramadan, I fast from the illusion of control
my prayers double
pleas for four white walls

*

my birthday comes and goes
I should be different already
I wonder, can she taste my wars

*

I drag the office to our moments
prop the paper legs of my self-esteem
please, God, keep her in the dream

*

her hand capes like a wild bat
my face bows
sculpt me, small hands

*

cobra in the crib
the terror of one's own power
smashing against an edge

*

what is the arithmetic to holding her
to transferring her unbroken
each night I break the equations

*

I move to the living room
she feasts on the new expanse
three trysts slim to one

*

all my love in a grind of teeth
her two inkwells pooling
everything in the leash of that whimper

the great green field

for Soma

here is the great green field
where at last I can remove the high heel of language
let the body supple in its meaning
her mouth my guide
it's the mouth I live for
that lives for me
her wail that shatters wild
small heart beasting out of cage
my animal wonder
every day

and if she purpled awake
not from my legs
but from the soft medicated sheet of men
and if my mouth sealed with each breaking
each violent crashing of the news
and if the year was marked by the believers
and the disbelievers
and if I believe will no one believe
in the name of God he thrust
into me
and if in her butoh tender hands I hang

shame
on language
that meats me pulverizes me
in public
revels in the republic
for whom I was not natural
so naturalized me
makes of her miracle
a mockery, life

before life
after which islands
better eaten by the sea

say, I see you
dare daughter
hear you
against all belief
brave this thin earth
devolving in the jaws
I dream you
perfectly personed
in body
embodied
least secret to yourself
the most sacred
you scare them
all free

Ghazal for Mothers & Tongues

It may be a broken, a shrill mother tongue,
But I'm raising my daughter in my ill mother tongue.

Translating Seuss and Nagara on the fly.
"Siya-o-safeyd" I'm fine, but at "zebra" I'm still, mother tongue.

The air is English, the water too.
How will you get past her gill, Mother Tongue?

Morning and night, I call Madar.
What's the word for guilt, mother or tongue?

A bat is a leather butterfly; turtle, a stone frog.
Dari, 1; English, nil. Mothertongue!!

We are writing our own kitab, you and I:
Oh, the Things They Try to Kill: mothers & tongues.

"Pappa climb zeena, get moon," she instructs.
I'm over the mahtab—each sprinkle of mother tongue.

Nafasem kee ast? I ask. *Soma Ali!* she beams.
In a word, my breath; and my dil, a mother's tongue.

a language entirely

She notices the shamal in the trees.
We call it *dancing.*
I wonder if I could teach her language—
entirely in metaphor.
This is a leaf yawning to the ground.
You have two starfish, right and left.
The clouds are playing piano again.

She already gets this.
Of the neighbor's umbrella on the balcony, tilted,
she says *khao.* Asleep.
Folds her hands under her ear,
head tilted.

To not correct.
To allow the pleasure of the construction.
Of the gesture.
How she distills.
For giraffe, she runs her hand
up her neck.
For elephant,
five fingers swing under her nose.

Her economy is expansive.
The same single syllable for multitudes:

> *Mah* for Madar jan
> *Mah* for maast
> for Marmite
> for cousin Mateen

We must train our ears to her tongue's subtleties.

She builds by repetition.
Reinforces by rhyme.

Soon "like" enters the room.
Sound to me like growling bear.
Look to me like window.
A wedge.
Approximate.
So begins a life of separation.

In February, she says plainly under our gasps:
Grass, trees, and barrf
like diamonds.
Stars, moon, and bed
like diamonds.

To see one in another
is to see as one another.

We watch her eyes
as much as her mouth.

Mucher, she corrects me.
I like ice cream mucher.
The robot lost its eye.
No, the robot is winking.

Because to say is to see.
The power of a tongue
accelerating,
revving repeatedly,
of teeth
marking the earth.

We listen with the hunger
of old eyes.

How Do You Laugh in Dari?

How do you say car in Dari?

How do you say umbrella?

She reaches my hip bone.

When I gently tug on her golden curl, it goes *boing,* a coil, like ع like غ.

My hair has always been straight and black. An ا.

It reaches my hip bone.

In Samarqand, we went to see the tomb of Daniel. It is 18 meters long. They say it grows five centimeters each year. It is still growing.

It's draped in green velvet with golden-threaded ayahs from the Qur'an.

Her hair is calligraphy I can't read.

How do you laugh in Dari? she asks with a straight face. Not an ا face. Her father's face.

This makes me laugh—and cry—at once.

We don't teach her Afrikaans, except for *biltong, lappie, baie dankie.*

At his former university, there are protests over the language policy.

Our language policy is to not teach the language of state violence and oppression.

Except we do.

I came to this country at three—the age my daughter is now. In preschool, I cried inconsolably. *They don't understand me.*

By fourth grade I replied to my parents only in English.

When my friend Ebony came over the first time, I said, *I'm sorry for the way my mother talks*. I meant, the calligraphy of her mouth.

All those years, no one asked us why we were here in the first place. They asked us other, petty things so that we would carry their shame instead.

The country's language policy works like most of its violences. Subtly. Supremely. Staunchly.

By college I wake up, mute and unrooted. *They don't understand me.*

I went to Berlin and asked a German to teach me my language, to show me photographs of her time in Kabul in the '60s. This made me laugh—and cry—at once. I copied her slides and said *tashakar* with an ۱ face.

At 24, I returned to Afghanistan with my father. At last. At first. Two decades later. When I opened my mouth, they widened their eyes. My father's eyes said, *I'm sorry for the way my daughter talks.*

Except I do and continue to. Sincerely. Scantily. Staunchly.

By two, she surpasses her father's Dari. By three, she replies only in English.

How do you say hegemony in Dari?

This country's language policy is draped in green velvet.

It is not mine to carry. Nor hers.

It's Nowruz. I am late to plant the sabza. She calls it *grass*. It's still growing. Seeds puckered and pushing through the dirt. She tugs on one of the tiny coils. *Look, Mamma, a C!*

I wake up to her joy—fluent and rooted.

Yes, I say, *for calligraphy,* for the golden threads of our mouths.

V. AFTER OCTOBER

counterparts

not all fear can be worked through
the ocean's example, constantly emptying

the nasturtiums, she instructed me, were edible
we ate the leaf, then the flower

despite his clouds, he believes in life
how we tire of one another's othering

I count the blessings
to keep from hurting him

the day circles
as a mosquito

when they lifted the cloth
I saw one that was not you

stood in my own corridor
and remarked the lack of windows

but I preferred to continually peel the orange and reject the fruit
wouldn't it taste of heartbreak

I was invited to take flight into the red road
to place my palm on the rock that formed the scripture

grief being vital
its violence being necessary

I rub the shadows
even in the garden

the prison of living by conviction
so many prisons

I will move more slowly
and it will still be a move

eyes of little night
and so, aching

his voice high-pitched and proving himself
back into my own body, eyes

I believe in doom and all its sister griefs
I believe in my thoughts reducing me to negligible

I believe in the words that I make up to color myself
we may not like you, but we love you in a very special way

embarrassed of my lines that grow out of ether
and die in ether

feel the light shrink
the breath small

may you inch in the direction of trust
hold the tail of your instinct

may you fail and get up to see
you did not die

may you expose your poems to the u/v
to the later atmospheres of your own doubt

arrive with the bow taut, and he notices
asks if it's pointed at him

I learned from my mother who left mines all across the house
the point was to startle us into guilt

imagine the future
as if your narrow divination could ever know

he and you will be two parallel lines
never touching

he will not leave
and you will punish him for that

what are the ways I try to be free
I wondered against the clock

a kind of life that is not certain
but alive

she spoke of fundamentalism
as *the understandable reaction to capitalist consumerism*

toys don't satisfy the question
why am I here

I look for another answer
my answer is *

how to make perfect?
seal every corner? edge God out?

the gnarled root of time
I touched it; it did not speak

the problem was always
trying to explain my face to everyone

here is my will: bright as a firecracker
here is his will: brighter

in the eye, notice the lake
in the lake, behold the sunken boats

in the boats are worms gnawing on the past
at the bottom of the past is the solid earth

the dream is that language

i am writing in a language my parents don't read.

i am writing a language my parents don't read.

•

listening to obama's eulogy for clementa pinckney at the AME. amazing grace. he sings. currents between the four of us watching. eyes running over.

how the ministers behind him nod and smile. through. so much history. now-story. what isn't stemmed, floods. rains. and reigns. bit the kid's eyes and caused torrents. all the violence that comes from a small place.

•

on train at 14th hear the harmonica through the open door. there are letters floating on her blouse: g, o, d. black on white. more churches burned. west 4th. tomorrow head to mountains. smokey. see the blue vein in the sky. father is free of it in the arm. all of us pooling on the phone. should he land on the ground now. press his toes in. recall the jasmine changing directions on its own.

•

in the field, r. imagines herself in 1830 carrying water. in 1850 being a baptist in a single room. 1863, ceasing faith. i imagine the cherokee in the hills. becoming unimaginable.

. . .

keep going interior. keep missing the arrival.

•

my mind doesn't work. it wants to kill me. i'd like it to kill me. press the breath out. flatten the little animal. all the air of thought, the bright spinning nowhere. snipe the eyes. coal the white of them.

•

stakes on the side of the road counting the miles. from coast to coast. the horizon meets itself in the aching zero.

•

home again or, in name. no lack of cataracts. my brain again. rather make a walk, a movie, see jacob lawrence show. make a life by conviction. in art, in nature.

•

he wakes naked. i wake clothed. he will swim. i will eat ravioli. declaratives help me through the dark.

•

no one knocking on the door. if being seen motivates. i am unmotivated. everyone throwing yarn online. i keep a quiet perimeter that suits me.

does it suit me?

•

and didn't we just finish *die unendliche geschichte?*

"denn jetzt wusste er: es gab in der welt tausend und tausend formen der freude, aber im grunde waren sie alle eine einzige, die freuden lieben zu können. beides war ein und dasselbe."

·

dream: i washed onto a far, dark island with my small turtle back. i struggled on the fine sand. night hurt. a wide cape. i could not lift the spear of the moon and cracked my shell.

. . .

as if the war is to say or not to say. no, the war is the illusion that there are only two. that everything can be reduced to two. the pain of separation. of being engulfed. of quiet. of quaking. the dream that there's a hole and something—one—a one—to slake the thirst.

•

trans-latina stories on the washington mall. ruby: "we could only be ourselves in clubs, in secluded spaces."

•

every landing an excuse to review, to regret, to pine for another way of being. i took my face against theirs. i lay it on the tracks.

let his poem bloom his way, and let mine alive a different way.

•

father's face is receding behind the insignificant day.

•

white phosphorous over raqqa. human flesh to the bone. organ failure. 2 children in nangarhar. 21 in iraq. a family market. aerial surveillance in southern somalia, the philippines. increased corporatization of pride. of patriotism. of a language that tallies. of one that doesn't.

•

the dream is that language is not inert.

•

mother's at camp lejeune translating murder. language is not inert.

. . .

yesterday in the sunlight but not in the sunlight. two places at once. sepehri: "my black stone is the sunlight in the flowers."

•

why can't i just go to my boss and use the word *suicide?*

•

shekast. shekastah. broken-line poetry.

"straight their figures, like alif."

•

seized as by smoke. morning, night. the mean carousel. the going nowhere. i am a fly to my own mind.

•

in the curl of the hair. the smoothing and turning and wrapping into a bun. to be as faithful, as lucid. in the slipping of earrings through the hole. the careful threading. arranging the blueberries and blackberries onto the spoon. the thoughtful gathering. lifting. bringing to lips. freedom must be in the crystal This.

Notebreaths

1. Noting the bud of the hibiscus whose clawed collar signals its wealth.

2. When it thunders. Nightly. Where to put one's weight. Eyes. Tongue. Yemen. Yangon. Minnesota.

3. Your quiet becomes pointed, a blade against your neighbor's skin.

4. At the hospital. The spread of magazines. *Traveler, Economist, Marie Claire.* "What's next for fashion?" "The puzzle of political Islam." The way the world worlds. Layers. Buries.

5. The Mother of All Bombs, misread as Bodies.

6. Language as an anchor in the white water, in the cascade.

7. When the body says it cannot any more. It cannot another. But something else insists. The body however and still. The body beneath the insistence surrenders. So with the past. What will not leave until it is seen, swallowed, passed through. History insists itself.

8. The hibiscus is native to tropical Africa. Its calyx is crushed into tea and juice. Is beaten into jelly. Its fibers coiled into rope.

9. Language as please. As please stop. As pleasing. As pleasant. Aspirational. Aspire. Inspire. Expire. Ex—

10. In the water, an alphabet

born of exile
      and which exiles—
extracts
          a child
   (from tongue)   (home)
an ex
   -love(d)
exhumes
        Father,
  (capital)
exactly
    never   exact

11. The rope is useful. Is used for "hunting, pulling, fastening, attaching, carrying, lifting, and climbing"

12. The point was to startle me into   my existence

NOTES

The Picture Tin
Is written after Charles Simic's "A Book Full of Pictures."

Salam Alaikum
Springs from conversations with my friend and former colleague Moussa Maiga on the shared edges of Afghan and Malian histories, cultures, and languages; it alternates between greetings in transliterated Dari (Farsi) and in Bambara.

A Secret Life in Misspelled Cities
Plays with the word "sher." In Dari, Panjsher Valley is دره پنجشیر (Dare-ye Panjsher) and translates to "valley of the five lions," where پنج (panj) is five and شعر (sher) is lion. The word for poem is the homophone شیر (sher).

washee / was she
Plays with the Dari word "washee" (وحشی), which means "savage" or "wild."

come baby
Draws inspiration and language from the *New York Times* article "With a Pregnant Iraqi, Collapsed in a Desert, as Bullets Fly" by Rukmini Callimachi, March 1, 2017.

Retreat
Includes excerpts from *A Journal of the Disasters in Afghanistan, 1841-2* (London: A. Spottiswoode), by Lady Sale, or Florentia Wynch, who was held captive for nine months during the first Anglo-Afghan War. The Brzezinksi quote is taken from a transcript of a 2010 interview between Zbigniew Kazimierz "Zbig" Brzezinski, President Jimmy Carter's National Security Advisor, and journalist Paul Jay. The larger quote is: "The fact is that even though we helped the Mujaheddin, they would have continued fighting without our help. . . . They didn't decide to fight because we urged them to. They're fighters, and they prefer to be independent. They just happen to have a curious complex: they don't like foreigners with guns in their country. And

they were going to fight the Soviets. But giving them Stingers was a very important forward step in defeating the Soviets, and that's all to the good as far as I'm concerned."

Zuihitsu for the New Diaspora
Is dedicated to my family and friends in Afghanistan and the new diaspora, for their bravery and for the unlanguageable.

Typical Fish
Refers to Peshmerga, (Kurdish: پێشمەرگە) which literally translates to "before death," as in "those who face death." The line "peh yaw sheen meem ray gawf hay" is the transliterated spelling of Peshmerga.

Rattling
Includes my slant translation of a line from "The Water's Footfall" by Sohrab Sepehri, from *The Water's Footfall / The Green Volume* by Sohrab Sepehri, translated by A. Zahedi and I. Salami (Tehran: Zabankadeh Publications).

Jan / Jahan
Plays with the words "jan" (جان), which means "dear" and "jahan" (جهان), which means "the world." "Padar jan" (جان پدر) is "dear father," a respectful address from a child to their father. "Jan-e Padar" (پدر جان) is "father's dear," a respectful address from a father to their child.

Brink
Quotes passages from Pema Chödrön's *When Things Fall Apart* (Boston: Shambhala Publications).

the dream is that language
Includes a passage in German from Michael Ende's *Die Unendliche Geschichte* (Stuttgart: K. Thienemanns Verlag).

"my black stone is the sunlight in the flowers" is adapted from the title poem from *Water's Footfall* by Sohrab Sepehri, translated from the Persian by Kazim Ali with Mohammad Jafar Mahallati (Richmond: Omnidawn Publishing).

"straight their figures, like alif" is adapted from a poem by Khushal Khan Khattak from *Afghan Poetry of the Seventeenth Century: Being Selections from the Poems of Khushhal Khan Khatak, with Translations and Grammatical Introductions*, by Khushal Khan Khattak, edited and compiled by C. E. Biddulph (London: K. Paul, Trench, Trübner & Co.).

ACKNOWLEDGMENTS

Grateful acknowledgement is given to the editors and staff of the following journals who first published some of these poems or their earlier iterations: *Arc Poetry Magazine, BOAAT Journal, Bone Bouquet, Brooklyn Rail, dOCUMENTA, Drunken Boat, Dusie, elsewhere literary magazine, Fourteen Hills, Green Mountains Review, HEArt Journal Online, KAF Journal, The Margins, The Muslim World, Newtown Literary, Origins Journal, Pinwheel Journal, Pocket Samovar,* and *Poetry Magazine.*

Several of these poems appeared in the chapbook *[G A T E S]*, published by Black Lawrence Press in 2017.

I feel immense gratitude to the many people and institutions that have shepherded this collection:

Teachers, friends, and fellows in community at the Afghan American Artists and Writers Association, Asian American Writers' Workshop, Bethany Arts Community, Blue Mountain Center, the Brooklyn College MFA program, Kundiman, Sustainable Arts Foundation, and in writing circles in friends' living rooms—for your tremendous help in refining these poems and enriching my reading, writing, and thinking.

Jenny Xie for being an early reader and helping shape and sharpen the whole, as well as for the deep generosity of time, friendship, and wisdom.

Naomi Shihab Nye for the gift of being seen and selected by a hero.

Aria Aber, Tina Chang, and Robin Coste Lewis for being both beacons and advocates.

Saadia Batool for lending use of the exquisite *A Thread to Map a Route* for the cover.

The University of Pittsburgh Press team for designing, editing, and welcoming the book with such care.

My deepest gratitude to my dearest friends for your sustaining and immeasurable love, for carrying me through many an October and more.

C. for always lovingly restoring me to the triangle.

My family from coast to coast and across oceans, with me you travel knowingly and unknowingly. Ali, Dirkie, Jawad, Jeff, Ria, Sahara, Shabnam, and Shaima, my daily nets.

Soma, Dari, and Nico: that we are each other's is All.